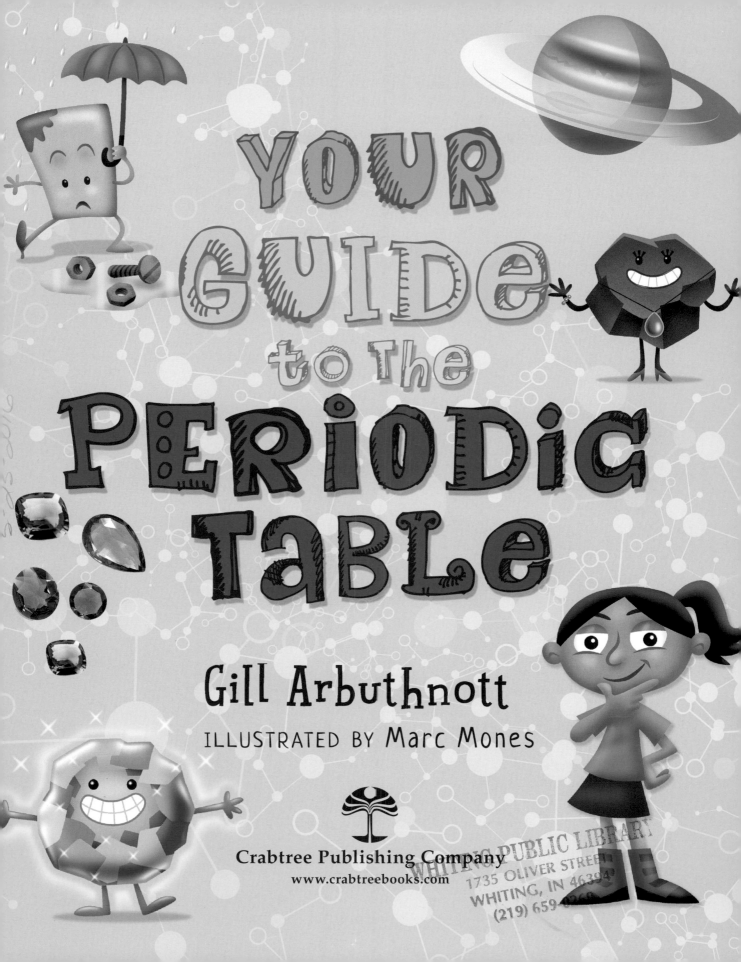

YOUR GUIDE to the PERIODIC TABLE

Gill Arbuthnott

ILLUSTRATED BY Marc Mones

Crabtree Publishing Company
www.crabtreebooks.com

Crabtree Publishing Company
www.crabtreebooks.com
1-800-387-7650

Published in Canada
Crabtree Publishing
616 Welland Avenue
St. Catharines, ON
L2M 5V6

Published in the United States
Crabtree Publishing
PMB 59051
350 Fifth Ave, 59th Floor
New York, NY 10118

Published by Crabtree Publishing Company in 2016

For Holly — Thank you!

Author: Gill Arbuthnott

Project coordinator: Kathy Middleton

Editor: Kathy Middleton

Proofreader: Janine Deschenes

Prepress technician: Tammy McGarr

Print and production coordinator:
  Margaret Amy Salter

Science Consultant: Shirley Duke

Text copyright © 2014 Gill Arbuthnott
Illustration copyright © 2014 Marc Mones

Additional picture acknowledgements:
Additional images all Shutterstock, aside from the following: p6 bottom © Wikimedia Commons, p7 top © Wikimedia Commons, p13 top © Wikimedia Commons, p13 top © Wikimedia Commons, p26 middle © Imperial War Museum/Wikimedia Commons, p44 top © Wikimedia Commons, p46 top © Wikimedia Commons, p50 bottom © Wikimedia Commons, p54 top left © Wikimedia Commons, p54 top right © Wikimedia Commons, p54 bottom © Wikimedia Commons.

First published in 2014 by A & C Black, an imprint of Bloomsbury Publishing Plc
Copyright © 2014 A & C Black

All Internet addresses given in this book were correct at the time of going to press. The author and publishers regret any incovenience caused if addresses have changed or if websites have ceased to exist, but can accept no responsibility for any such changes.

Printed in Canada/022016/MA20151130

Library and Archives Canada Cataloguing in Publication

Arbuthnott, Gill, author
     Your guide to the periodic table / Gill Arbuthnott ; Marc Mones, illustrator.

(Drawn to science, illustrated guides to key science concepts)
Includes index.
ISBN 978-0-7787-2245-8 (bound).--ISBN 978-0-7787-2253-3 (paperback)

     1. Periodic table of the elements--Juvenile literature. 2. Chemical elements--Juvenile literature. I. Mones, Marc, illustrator II. Title.

QD467.A73 2016   j546'.8   C2015-907108-9

Library of Congress Cataloging-in-Publication Data

Names: Arbuthnott, Gill, author. | Mones, Marc, illustrator.
Title: Your guide to the periodic table / Gill Arbuthnott ; illustrated by
   Marc Mones.
Description: Crabtree Publishing Company, 2016. | Series: Drawn to
   science : illustrated guides to key science concepts | Includes index.
Identifiers: LCCN 2015042100| ISBN 9780778722458 (reinforced library
   binding : alk. paper) | ISBN 9780778722533 (pbk. : alk. paper)
Subjects: LCSH: Periodic table of the elements--Juvenile literature. |
   Chemical elements--Juvenile literature.
Classification: LCC QD467 .A73 2016 | DDC 546/.8--dc23
LC record available at http://lccn.loc.gov/2015042100

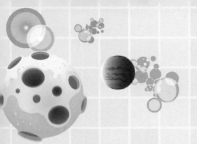

Contents

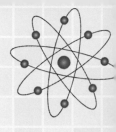

Introduction

How many different building blocks does it take to make a single cell? Or a stone? Or a star? You may think it would be hundreds or even thousands, but it's actually far fewer.

It shouldn't really be such a surprise. After all, think how many different creations you can make from only a few toy building blocks. The building blocks of the universe are called elements. There are only 92 of them, but there are millions of possible combinations you can make with them.

Did you know there is a metal that screams when you bend it? Or that one is so **reactive**, it can make glass burst into flames? How would you like to know which are the most poisonous elements, and which ones are the most radioactive?

Well, read on...

What Are the Elements?

An element is a substance, or material that is made up of tiny pieces of matter called atoms. An element can contain only one type of atom. It can't be broken down into a simpler substance. There are 92 different elements that occur naturally. Others can be made in a laboratory by chemists. Some of these human-made elements do occur naturally, but only in tiny amounts. In this book, we're going to stick with just the original 92 elements.

Chemists started to identify elements hundreds of years ago. By the middle of the 1800s, 57 were known. Nobody could agree on how they should be grouped together. Someone needed to take charge and sort things out...

This was a job for Professor Mendeleev.

Dmitri Mendeleev

was born in 1834 in Siberia, in Russia. He was the youngest of 14—possibly even 17—children! When Mendeleev grew up, he taught chemistry at St. Petersburg University. Some believe he is responsible for bringing the metric system to Russia. In photos he looks like a real mad scientist—it was said he cut his hair and beard only once a year!

Reihen	Gruppo I. $R'O$	Gruppo II. RO	Gruppo III. R^2O^3	Gruppo IV. RH^4 RO^2	Gruppo V. RH^3 R^2O^5	Gruppo VI. RH^2 RO^3	Gruppo VII. RH R^2O^7	Gruppo VIII. RO^4
1	H=1							
2	Li=7	Be=9,4	B=11	C=12	N	O=16	F=19	
3	Na=23	Mg=24	Al=27,3	Si=	P=31	S=	Cl=35,5	
4	K=39	Ca=40	—=44	Ti=48	=51	Cr=52	=55	Fe=56, Co=59, Ni=59, Cu=63.
5	(Cu=63)	Zn=65	—=68		As=75	S=	r=80	
6	Rb=85	Sr=87	?Yt=88	Zr=	=94	Mo=96	So=	Ru=104, Rh=104, Pd=106, Ag=108.
7	(Ag=108)	Cd=112	In=113				=127	
8	Cs=133	Ba=137	?Di=138	?Ce=				
9		(~)						
10	—	—	—	?Er=178	?La=1			Os=195, Ir=197, Pt=198, Au=199.
11	(Au=199)	Hg=200	Tl=204	Pb=207				
12	—	—	—	Th=231				

Professor Mendeleev's periodic table

Professor Mendeleev's chemistry class

Mendeleev had a brilliant idea during his career. He arranged the elements in a chart based on their weights and their properties, or characteristics. He called his arrangement the periodic table.

Mendeleev found that when he arranged the elements in this way, there seemed to be "families" of elements that shared similarities. He also discovered gaps in the table where no known element fit the pattern. Mendeleev predicted that new elements would eventually be found to fill these gaps. He even predicted the weights and properties they would have.

Mendeleev's predictions helped other chemists to find the missing elements, and he was proven correct.

7

How the Periodic Table Works

The color of each box tells you if the element is a metal, a non-metal, or a **metalloid**. The rows in the table are called periods. When you read from left to right across a period, the atomic numbers of the elements increase. The columns of the table are called groups. The elements in a group have similar properties. The atomic weight, or mass, of the elements increases, or gets heavier, when you read a group from top to bottom.

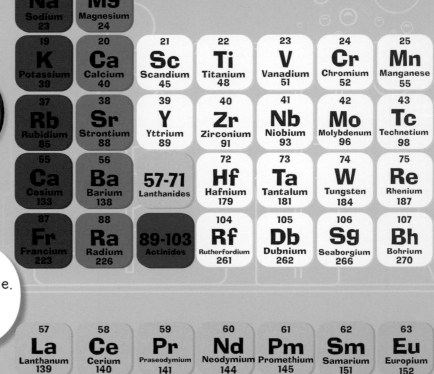

1 H Hydrogen 1						
3 Li Lithium 7	4 Be Beryllium 9					
11 Na Sodium 23	12 Mg Magnesium 24					
19 K Potassium 39	20 Ca Calcium 40	21 Sc Scandium 45	22 Ti Titanium 48	23 V Vanadium 51	24 Cr Chromium 52	25 Mn Manganese 55
37 Rb Rubidium 85	38 Sr Strontium 88	39 Y Yttrium 89	40 Zr Zirconium 91	41 Nb Niobium 93	42 Mo Molybdenum 96	43 Tc Technetium 98
55 Ca Cesium 133	56 Ba Barium 138	57-71 Lanthanides	72 Hf Hafnium 179	73 Ta Tantalum 181	74 W Tungsten 184	75 Re Rhenium 187
87 Fr Francium 223	88 Ra Radium 226	89-103 Actinides	104 Rf Rutherfordium 261	105 Db Dubnium 262	106 Sg Seaborgium 266	107 Bh Bohrium 270

57 La Lanthanum 139	58 Ce Cerium 140	59 Pr Praseodymium 141	60 Nd Neodymium 144	61 Pm Promethium 145	62 Sm Samarium 151	63 Eu Europium 152
89 Ac Actinium 227	90 Th Thorium 232	91 Pa Protactinium 231	92 U Uranium 238	93 Np Neptunium 237	94 Pu Plutonium 244	95 Am Americium 243

Here is the modern periodic table. Let's take a closer look...

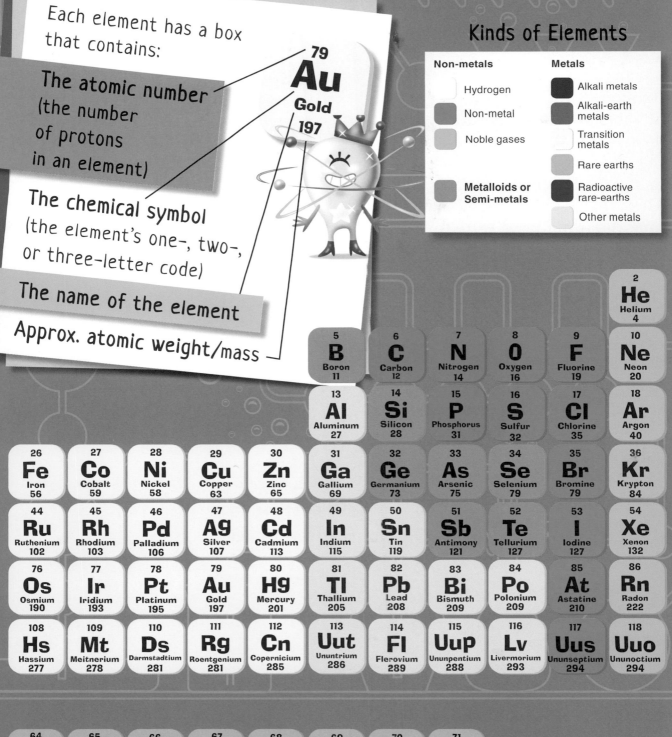

Each element has a box that contains:

The atomic number
(the number of protons in an element)

The chemical symbol
(the element's one-, two-, or three-letter code)

The name of the element

Approx. atomic weight/mass

79
Au
Gold
197

Kinds of Elements

Non-metals	Metals
Hydrogen	Alkali metals
Non-metal	Alkali-earth metals
Noble gases	Transition metals
	Rare earths
Metalloids or Semi-metals	Radioactive rare-earths
	Other metals

2 He Helium 4

5 B Boron 11	6 C Carbon 12	7 N Nitrogen 14	8 O Oxygen 16	9 F Fluorine 19	10 Ne Neon 20
13 Al Aluminum 27	14 Si Silicon 28	15 P Phosphorus 31	16 S Sulfur 32	17 Cl Chlorine 35	18 Ar Argon 40

26 Fe Iron 56	27 Co Cobalt 59	28 Ni Nickel 58	29 Cu Copper 63	30 Zn Zinc 65	31 Ga Gallium 69	32 Ge Germanium 73	33 As Arsenic 75	34 Se Selenium 79	35 Br Bromine 79	36 Kr Krypton 84
44 Ru Ruthenium 102	45 Rh Rhodium 103	46 Pd Palladium 106	47 Ag Silver 107	48 Cd Cadmium 113	49 In Indium 115	50 Sn Tin 119	51 Sb Antimony 121	52 Te Tellurium 127	53 I Iodine 127	54 Xe Xenon 132
76 Os Osmium 190	77 Ir Iridium 193	78 Pt Platinum 195	79 Au Gold 197	80 Hg Mercury 201	81 Tl Thallium 205	82 Pb Lead 208	83 Bi Bismuth 209	84 Po Polonium 209	85 At Astatine 210	86 Rn Radon 222
108 Hs Hassium 277	109 Mt Meitnerium 278	110 Ds Darmstadtium 281	111 Rg Roentgenium 281	112 Cn Copernicium 285	113 Uut Ununtrium 286	114 Fl Flerovium 289	115 Uup Ununpentium 288	116 Lv Livermorium 293	117 Uus Ununseptium 294	118 Uuo Ununoctium 294

64 Gd Gadolinium 158	65 Tb Terbium 159	66 Dy Dysprosium 163	67 Ho Holmium 165	68 Er Erbium 168	69 Tm Thulium 169	70 Yb Ytterbium 174	71 Lu Lutetium 175	Lanthanides
96 Cm Curium 247	97 Bk Berkelium 247	98 Cf Californium 251	99 Es Einsteinium 252	100 Fm Fermium 257	101 Md Mendelevium 258	102 No Nobelium 259	103 Lr Lawrencium 262	Actinides

Atoms

An atom is the smallest unit of an element. Atoms are so incredibly small—just 0.000001 millimeters—that they can only be seen by using a very special microscope. Their tiny size is very hard to imagine—and most of that size is empty space!

The nucleus, or center, of an atom is made up of **protons** and **neutrons**. A proton is a tiny particle that has a positive charge, and neutrons are tiny particles with no charge. These make up almost all of the atom's mass. **Electrons** are particles that have a negative charge that is equal to the protons' positive charge. Electrons whiz around outside the nucleus.

If the whole atom was the size of a soccer field, the nucleus would be the size of a marble, and the electrons would be like tiny insects buzzing around the marble's edge. The rest is just…nothing!

Here's how atoms are often shown:

electrons = negative charge

nucleus (protons = positive charge, and neutrons = no charge)

Let's try to understand this a different way...

Compounds and mixtures

Most substances in the world are either **compounds** or **mixtures**. Compounds are made up of atoms that have two or more elements joined together to form **molecules**. For example, an oxygen atom joined to two hydrogen atoms makes a molecule of water.

Air, on the other hand, is a mixture. It is made up of various elements, such as oxygen and nitrogen, as well as compounds, such as carbon dioxide. They all move around together without actually being joined to each other.

Think of a mixture as a box of building blocks. The blocks are inside the box, but they're not joined together. Building blocks that are joined to each other are a compound.

Solids, liquids, and gases

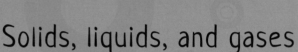

These are known as the states, or forms, of matter. Chemists used to think that there were only three states—solids, liquids, and gases. Most things exist in one of these forms. However, there is a fourth state that is fairly common called plasma, as well as many other forms called "exotic" states of matter. These exist only in extreme laboratory conditions, or are only a theory, or idea.

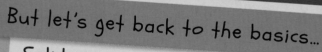

But let's get back to the basics...

Solids have a fixed shape and volume. The molecules are tightly packed, which means they can't move around—but they do vibrate.

Liquids have a fixed volume, but take the shape of the container they are in. The molecules are tightly packed but can move more than they can in a solid.

Gases have no fixed volume or shape. The molecules are not tightly packed and can move around freely.

Bang! The Story Begins...

Once upon a time, there was no universe at all—no space, no time, nothing. Then a tiny point in space, called a singularity, appeared. It was unbelievably hot and its molecules were tightly packed.

Eventually, about 13.7 billion years ago, the singularity exploded with unimaginable force and began to expand incredibly fast. Physicists now call this the Big Bang. As the singularity expanded, it became less hot and packed.

This caused space and time to come into existence, and the universe was born. At its beginning point, there were no elements—not even stars or planets. All that existed were **subatomic** particles, which were tiny things that would eventually form atoms. It took hundreds of thousands of years for the first atoms to form. Eventually, the first two elements formed: hydrogen and helium. Let's start with them and work our way from the lightest to the heaviest elements in the periodic table.

Atomic number 1

H
Hydrogen
Non-Metal

Hydrogen is the lightest element. Its atoms each contain only one proton and one electron. It is also the most common element. At least 90% of all the atoms in the universe are hydrogen.

Hydrogen was one of the first elements created after the Big Bang. It is lighter than air and was used to fill airships for air travel. Recently, we have begun to burn hydrogen as a fuel in cars and buses. Burning hydrogen produces no pollution and is cleaner than burning **fossil fuels** such as oil and gasoline.

The Hindenberg disaster

Airships filled with hydrogen were known as zeppelins. By 1910, they were used regularly to carry passengers. They were also used by the German army to drop bombs on London during World War I. Passenger flights across the Atlantic Ocean started in the 1920s. However, on May 6, 1937, disaster struck when the Hindenberg airship burned and crashed in New Jersey. Flying from Frankfurt, the crash killed 35 of the 97 people on board. It was the end of airship travel. It was assumed for a long time that the crash was caused by burning hydrogen, but now there are other theories. One theory is that flammable paint on the airship's outer covering was the first thing to catch fire, and that the hydrogen started burning after that.

Crash of the Hindenburg in New Jersey, May 1937

Burning stars

The Sun is made mostly of hydrogen. Sunlight is the visible energy released when hydrogen is turned into helium by a process called nuclear fusion. This process releases huge amounts of energy.

13

Helium was first **discovered in space** in 1868. In 1882, a scientist studying lava from Mount Vesuvius in Italy identified it on Earth. Created in the Big Bang, helium is lighter than air. That is why party balloons filled with helium float.

Although it is the second-most **abundant** element, making up almost one quarter of the universe's mass, helium is quite rare on Earth. Most of it comes from natural gas—a resource Earth is running out of! Helium's molecules are so tiny that whenever any are released, they float off into space. Helium is also used in the manufacturing of cell phones and computer chips, as a super coolant in the **Large Hadron Collider**, and as part of the gas mixture in the breathing tanks of deep-sea divers.

Dangerous helium

Breathing in helium from a party balloon can be dangerous. It is often portrayed as a harmless trick that makes a person's voice sound squeaky. However, doctors and even gas companies warn against this practice.

Why does it change the voice? It's because the sound waves made by the vibration of the vocal cords are traveling through helium instead of air. Because helium is much lighter than air, the waves travel faster through it. The faster speed of the voice's sound waves changes how they sound.

Helium is dangerous because it replaces the air in the lungs the same way that water does when a person is drowning. It cuts off the oxygen supply.

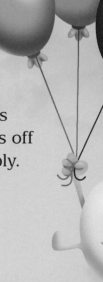

The Noble Gases

Non-metals

These are the elements in the same column, or group of the periodic table, as helium. They are:

Neon	Ne	Atomic number 10
Argon	Ar	Atomic number 18
Krypton	Kr	Atomic number 36
Xenon	Xe	Atomic number 54
Radon	Rn	Atomic number 86

10
Ne
Neon

18
Ar
Argon

36
Kr
Krypton

54
Xe
Xenon

86
Rn
Radon

The elements in the table above are called the noble gases. They are **nonreactive** to other elements. This means they rarely join with any other elements to make compounds. In fact, neon doesn't form any chemical compounds at all. It's kind of like how the **noble** classes in the Middle Ages wouldn't mix with the lower classes.

Noble gases are used in various types of lighting. Argon was used in old-fashioned light bulbs and is still used in fluorescent tubes.

The gases have medical uses, too. Xenon is used to numb pain, and radioactive radon is used as a cancer treatment.

Krypton and Kryptonite

Don't confuse krypton with Kryptonite! Kryptonite is a fictional element from Superman's home planet of Krypton. It drains him of his superpowers. In real life, krypton is just a gas, not a planet!

Atomic number 6

C
Carbon
Non-Metal

All life on Earth is based on chemicals that contain carbon. Carbon can join with other elements to form millions of different compounds. Pure carbon can exist in several different forms: graphite (the "lead" in pencils), diamonds, buckyballs (tiny spheres of graphite), and graphene (a layer of graphite that is one atom thick). Scientists are very excited about graphene because it is strong, light, almost transparent, and conducts, or carries, both heat and electricity very well.

H Mg Ne K He

Diamond

Diamond is the hardest, naturally occurring material. Most diamonds are mined in Africa. The largest diamond ever found was the Cullinan diamond, which weighed over 21 ounces (600 g)! It was cut into over 100 smaller diamonds. Some of them are now part of the Crown Jewels, belonging to the Queen of England.

The scientific name of the diamond star is BPM 37093. What a mouthful!

The diamond star

Astronomers have found the very compact remains of a massive, collapsed star. Like a diamond, it is made mostly of crystalized carbon. This space diamond may be five times the size of Earth!

Climate change

Fossil fuels such as coal, gas, and oil were originally living things, so they contain a lot of carbon. When we burn them, they release carbon dioxide gas. This gas collects in the atmosphere and traps extra heat from the sun there. This is known as the Greenhouse Effect, and most scientists believe it is causing harmful **climate change**.

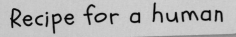

Recipe for a human

Which elements are you made of? How much of each one do you need to make a human?

A 155-pound (70 kg) adult is mostly made up of:

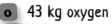

O	43 kg oxygen
C	16 kg carbon
H	7 kg hydrogen
N	1.8 kg nitrogen
Ca	1 kg calcium
P	780 g phosphorus
K	140 g potassium
S	140 g sulphur
Na	100 g sodium
Cl	95 g chlorine
Mg	19 g magnesium
Fe	4.2 g iron
F	2.6 g fluorine
Zn	2.3 g zinc
Si	1.0 g silicon

N
Nitrogen
Non-Metal

Almost 80% of the air around us is made up of nitrogen. We breathe it in and out, but we don't actually use it for anything in our bodies. It is vital, however, as a fertilizer, or food, for plant growth. Plants take in nitrogen after it has been changed into a different form. Farmers add artificially-made fertilizer to soil to help plants grow.

Liquid nitrogen has a temperature of –320 degrees Fahrenheit (–196 degrees Celsius). If you put a banana into liquid nitrogen, it will freeze so hard that you can use it to hammer a nail into a wooden board! It is used (liquid nitrogen, that is, not a frozen banana) to keep foods frozen when being transported long distances.

Explosives

Many explosives contain nitrogen. Nitroglycerine is a highly explosive liquid. Swedish chemist Alfred Nobel used it to invent a more stable explosive called dynamite in 1867. Azide is a nitrogen-based explosive used to save lives—it forms the gas that quickly inflates airbags in cars. With the money he made from his invention, Nobel founded the Nobel Prizes, given out each year to people who make extraordinary discoveries or perform acts that benefit humankind.

Laughing gas

Nitrous oxide is a gas. It is used during surgery as an anesthetic, which is something given to numb a patient's senses so they don't feel pain. Also known as laughing gas, it has the effect of making some people giggle.

Be
Beryllium
Metal

This is an uncommon element because it can only be generated by a supernova, or giant exploding star. It can be found as crystals of the **ore** beryllium, up to 19.5-feet (6 m) long!

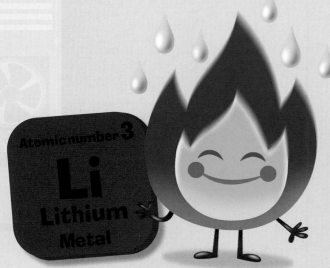

Atomic number 3

Li
Lithium
Metal

Atomic number 5

B
Boron
Non-Metal

Lithium was the third element created by the Big Bang. It's the lightest metal, and is very reactive. That means it transforms easily when it comes into contact with another material. For example, it can burst into flames when it comes into contact with water and oxygen. It has to be stored safely under oil or coated in petroleum jelly.

Boron is the lightest metalloid. Its mixture of properties makes it very useful. Without boron, there could be no Silly Putty, fireworks would be missing a shade of green, and Queen Elizabeth I of England would have been without her favorite white makeup. Boron is always found combined with other elements. Used for hundreds of years, it wasn't until 1892 that American chemist Ezekiel Weintraub was able to identify the properties of pure boron.

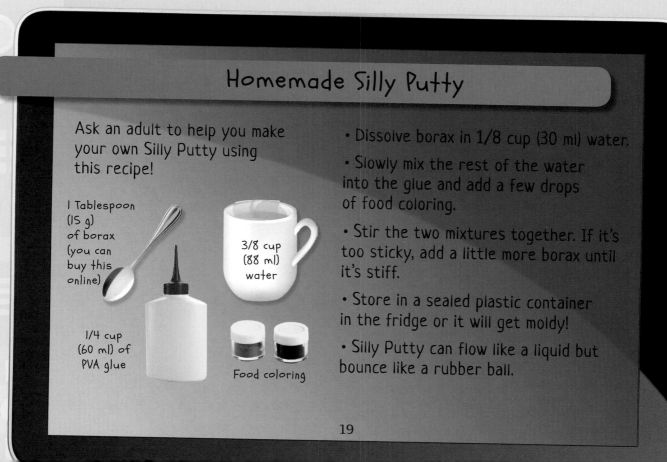

Homemade Silly Putty

Ask an adult to help you make your own Silly Putty using this recipe!

1 Tablespoon (15 g) of borax (you can buy this online)

3/8 cup (88 ml) water

1/4 cup (60 ml) of PVA glue

Food coloring

• Dissolve borax in 1/8 cup (30 ml) water.

• Slowly mix the rest of the water into the glue and add a few drops of food coloring.

• Stir the two mixtures together. If it's too sticky, add a little more borax until it's stiff.

• Store in a sealed plastic container in the fridge or it will get moldy!

• Silly Putty can flow like a liquid but bounce like a rubber ball.

Atomic number 8

O
Oxygen
Non-Metal

Oxygen is the most common element on Earth. It makes up 20% of every breath you take. Oxygen is needed to burn fuel such as coal or gasoline in order to release the energy they contain. This happens in your body, too. Your cells use the oxygen you breathe in to release energy from the food you eat.

When Earth first formed, there was no oxygen in the atmosphere. Most of it was made when plants evolved and began to produce it by the process of **photosynthesis**.

Here are some things I bet you didn't know about oxygen.

Sun

Ozone layer

Earth

Ozone: Up high, down low

Most oxygen molecules are made of two oxygen atoms. Some are made of three atoms and are called ozone molecules. They create a thin layer high up in the atmosphere about 12.5 miles (20 km) above Earth. This layer of ozone protects us by absorbing 90% of the **ultraviolet (UV) radiation** in sunlight that is harmful to humans. Unfortunately, the ozone layer has been getting thinner due to pollution from human activity. The damage has been slowing down since some chemicals have been banned. So, is ozone always a good thing? No. On hot, sunny days, ozone close to ground level increases. It makes breathing harder, especially for people with asthma and bronchitis. It can also damage plant leaves.

Northern lights

Also known as the aurora borealis, the northern lights are spectacular bands of colorful light that appear in the sky during the right atmospheric conditions. When **cosmic rays** from the Sun interact with oxygen molecules in Earth's outer atmosphere, curtains of green or crimson light move around as the rays are pulled by Earth's magnetic field. The best places to see them are Iceland, Greenland, Alaska, and in the northern parts of Canada, Norway, and Finland.

Helpful or harmful?

We all need oxygen to survive, but pure oxygen can be dangerous. Babies born before their lungs were fully developed used to be given pure oxygen to breathe inside **incubators**. In 1954, opthamologist Dr. Arnall Patz connected a rise in blindness in babies to incubators. He discovered that high concentrations of oxygen can cause abnormal growth of the blood vessels in the retina at the back of the eye, causing blindness.

Northern lights, seen from Alaska

Atomic number 9

F
Fluorine
Non-Metal

Pure fluorine is a pale yellow gas but, in nature, it's always found as part of a compound. There are things containing fluorine all over your house. It's in the fluoride in toothpaste, which helps keep teeth strong—although too much will turn them brown. Waterproof materials used in raincoats are also made with fluorine.

You wouldn't want to run into fluorine as a gas, however. It is so reactive it will make almost anything—even glass—burst into flames!

Atomic number 11

Na
Sodium
Metal

Sodium compounds give the ocean its salty taste. We add sodium chloride, or salt, to food to give it flavor. Your body uses sodium to send signals through your nervous system. Precious in ancient times, some believe the word "**salary**" came from the practice of giving money to Roman soldiers to buy salt.

Salinas Grandes, Salt desert, Argentina Andes

Crystals

Crystals are solids in which molecules are arranged in a highly organized, **3-D** pattern. Sodium chloride is a crystal, and so are diamonds and snowflakes. Crystals have flat faces called facets, with sharp edges. How would you like to grow your own crystals?

> If only you could grow diamond crystals as easily as salt.

Growing salt crystals

You will need:

1/4 cup (60 ml) of salt

1 cup (235 ml) boiling water

A piece of sponge (bath, not cake!)

2 teaspoons (10 ml) of vinegar

Food coloring (optional)

• Get an adult to help you mix the boiling water, salt, vinegar, and food coloring (if you're using it), and stir well.

• Put the sponge in a shallow dish.

• Pour enough mixture over the sponge in order to soak it completely and cover the bottom of the dish. Keep the rest for later.

• Leave the dish on a windowsill or somewhere warm and airy. Crystals should start to form within 24 hours.

• As the liquid in the dish evaporates, add more mixture and see how big you can get the crystals to grow.

Atomic number 12

Mg
Magnesium
Metal

Plants need magnesium to perform the process of photosynthesis, or making their own food. Humans need it to prevent our bones from becoming brittle. Plants take in magnesium compounds from soil through their roots. Obviously we can't do the same, so we have to eat it. The good news? Chocolate is a good source of magnesium!

Magnesium burns with an intense white light and was once used in photographic flashbulbs. It was also used for destructive purposes in World War II, to make bombs that would set enemy cities on fire.

Atomic number 13

Al
Aluminum
Metal

Aluminum is the most common metal on Earth. Yet, when it was first discovered in the 1800s, it was more expensive than gold! This was because it was very difficult to separate it from the minerals in which it was found. Now that an easy method has been discovered, lightweight aluminum is used to make everything from soft drink cans, to car bodies, to bikes.

Aluminum is also a good **conductor**, or carrier, of heat and is used to make cooking foil. It's also a good reflector of heat. It is used in spacecrafts to protect the vehicles from the Sun's heat. It takes a lot of energy to make aluminum, so it's a very good idea to recycle it.

Atomic number 14

Si
Silicon
Non-Metal

Most soil and rock have a lot of silicon in them. Lots of precious and semi-precious stones such as emerald, jade, and amethyst also contain silicon. Silicon is used to make everything from bricks and glass to computer chips and solar panels.

Silicon chips

Silicon chips are the control centers of many electronic devices such as your cell phone and computer—even your microwave. The invention of the silicon chip, or integrated circuit, was a huge step forward in electronic technology. Chips were cheap to make and very complex circuits could fit into a tiny space. The first silicon integrated circuit was developed in 1959.

Arrowheads

In the Stone Age, the first tools made by humans, such as knives and arrowheads, were made from flint. A compound of silicon and oxygen, flint was useful because it could be easily split to give very sharp edges.

Silicon chip for a computer

Today's chips can contain millions-of-times more information than the first versions.

Atomic number 15

P
Phosphorus
Non-Metal

Phosphorus was the first element to be discovered in modern times —1669 to be exact. It was first identified in human urine by a German **alchemist** who was trying to discover how to turn other metals into gold. (It's impossible, by the way.) Phosphorus is highly **toxic**, or poisonous, but your body has a lot of it in the form of calcium phosphate—the main ingredient in bones and teeth.

Damaged city of Hamburg

It is very reactive, which is why it's used to make match heads. In World War II, burning phosphorus was dropped on the German city of Hamburg by the countries who fought against Nazi Germany. Most of the city was destroyed.

Atomic number 16

S
Sulfur
Non-Metal

Sulfur is a bright yellow non-metal. It is made during volcanic eruptions, both on land and on the seabed. It used to be called Brimstone, which means "burnstone." Sulfur itself doesn't smell, but a lot of sulfur compounds do. They give garlic, mustard, cabbage, and skunks their smell.

Skunk smell

A skunk's spray can temporarily blind you. It makes your eyes water, and can cause nausea and breathing difficulties for people with asthma. It's very difficult to get rid of the smell. By the way, a bath in tomato juice doesn't really get rid of the smell of a skunk's spray. It just masks, or covers, the smell.

Sulfa drugs

Medicines made from sulfur have been used for hundreds of years. Brimstone and treacle (now known as sulfur and molasses) was a popular treatment for constipation in the 1800s. Today, sulfa-based drugs are still used to treat digestive problems.

Gunpowder

Gunpowder is a mixture of sulfur, charcoal, and saltpeter, or potassium nitrate. When it was first made, it had to be smashed into a powder by hammer. Not a great job—it would often explode! Now, gunpowder is mainly used in fireworks.

Mustard gas

Mustard gas is a poisonous, deadly gas that contains sulfur. Breathing it in damages the cells lining the lungs. Mustard gas was used as a weapon during World War I and was officially banned from use in warfare in 1925.

Atomic number 17

Cl
Chlorine
Non-Metal

Chlorine was originally given the much less snappy name of "dephlogisticated muriatic acid air" when it was first described in the 1630s. However, it had been known and used for thousands of years—most commonly in the form of sodium chloride, or salt.

Most disinfectants and bleaches are chlorine compounds. Drinking water in many countries is treated with chlorine to kill germs. It has helped wipe out diseases like typhoid and cholera. However, chlorine can also be deadly. Chlorine gas was also used as a poison in the trenches of World War I.

Atomic number 19

K

Potassium
Metal

Why K? It's from the medieval Latin word *kalium*, which is potash, or the ashes of plants. Potassium was first **isolated** from potash.

It has many uses, including as a fertilizer and a meat preservative. It's also important in helping our nerves work properly. If you sweat a lot, you can lose so much potassium that you get cramps and muscle weakness. Fortunately, you can easily replace missing potassium by eating a banana—not surprisingly, the snack of choice for many athletes.

Atomic number 20

Ca

Calcium
Metal

Calcium is a silvery metal, but most of the things you will come across that contain calcium are white. Examples include chalk, bones, and teeth. Bones and teeth are made of calcium phosphate, and chalk is made from calcium carbonates, which are the skeletons of billions of tiny, long-dead organisms.

The expression "to be in the limelight" now refers to being the center of attention in the public eye.

In the early days of theater, the stage effect of lightning was created by aiming a hydrogen flame at calcium oxide, also called lime. This effect was called limelight.

Atomic number 21

Sc
Scandium
Metal

Scandium is one of the elements that Mendeleev predicted should exist. It was discovered ten years after his prediction. It only occurs in tiny amounts in Earth's crust, so it wasn't until 1937 that someone managed to produce a lump of it. Adding tiny amounts to aluminum makes a very strong **alloy**, used to make aircraft.

Atomic number 22

Ti
Titanium
Metal

Titanium is a very strong, but light metal. It won't rust away in seawater like iron, so it is often used to make submarine hulls. It is also used to make artificial hip joints, as well as the pins and plates that are sometimes used to mend broken bones. It is named after the Titans—a race of giants in Greek mythology.

Atomic number 24

Cr
Chromium
Metal

Although it is a silvery white metal, chromium is what gives emeralds and rubies their colors. It is used as a rust-proof plating on steel and gives classic cars their shiny bumpers.

Atomic number 23

V
Vanadium
Metal

Another very strong but light metal, vanadium was used in the steel alloy of the first mass-produced car: the Model T Ford.

Model T Ford

29

Atomic number 26

Fe
Iron
Metal

Iron is the most widely used metal. The Iron Age began 3,000 years ago when people learned to smelt, or process, iron from iron ore. It also could have come from meteorites that landed from space! Blacksmiths were regarded as being almost magical because they could turn rock into metal.

Here are some more amazing facts about iron.

King Arthur

In the legend, King Arthur proves he is the rightful king by "drawing forth the sword from the stone and anvil." Illustrations usually show Arthur pulling a sword from a big stone and a blacksmith's anvil, which is a block that hot steel is hammered on. However, some think the phrase refers to hammering stone (ore) into a sword on an anvil. Was King Arthur a blacksmith?

Rust

Iron is very reactive. One unwelcome result of this is that it will **corrode**, or break down, if it is not protected by paint or **galvanized** with a coating of zinc. This corrosion, or rust, is a compound called hydrated iron oxide. You can see this process for yourself if you put an iron or steel nail in a dish of water. It should start to rust in a few days.

Blood

In your blood there are millions of tiny red blood cells. They are full of a chemical called hemoglobin, which allows the cells to carry oxygen. Hemoglobin contains iron.

If you don't get enough iron in your diet, your blood can't carry enough oxygen.

Atomic number 25

Mn
Manganese
Metal

Most manganese is found on the seabed in the form of nodules. In the same way that a pearl forms around a piece of grit in an oyster, nodules are lumps of manganese minerals that form around a central particle. Manganese is used to remove iron compounds in glass making. The result is a very clear glass. It was also used many thousands of years ago by the earliest artists. The black color in cave paintings is manganese oxide.

Atomic number 28

Ni
Nickel
Metal

Nickel is one of the four magnetic elements. (The other three are iron, cobalt, and gadolinium.) Nickel is often used in coins, which is why the five-cent coin is known as a nickel. It's also used to make cheap jewelry, especially earrings, although some people can become allergic to it.

The nodules of manganese are the size of potatoes.

Atomic number 27

Co
Cobalt
Metal

Cobalt is named after the German word *kobald*, which means goblin, because the German miners who discovered it in the 1500s thought it was cursed! Cobalt chloride can be used to make invisible ink. You can write a secret message in invisible ink, then write a fake letter on top of it with ordinary ink. When you heat the paper, the invisible message appears, as if by magic…

Atomic number 29

Cu
Copper
Metal

Copper has been used for thousands of years. It is often combined with other metals to make into alloys. The Bronze Age, which began 5,000 years ago, was named after the alloy, bronze. Bronze was created by combining copper and tin. It was used then to make weapons, coins, and jewelry. Today, copper is used in electrical wires and printed circuit boards. Outdoors, it changes over time to a green finish called verdigris. That's why the Statue of Liberty in New York appears green.

Atomic number 30

Zn
Zinc
Metal

Zinc is vital for health, and according to research, two billion people don't get enough of it. In areas where there isn't enough zinc in the soil, crops don't grow properly. Maple syrup is a very rich source.

Atomic number 31

Ga
Gallium
Metal

Gallium is a metal which melts at just 86° F (30° C). You could hold it in your hand and watch it melt! Chemists who like practical jokes have been known to make teaspoons out of it, which melt when you stir your tea. Gallium compounds are also used in cell phones and computers. Gallium nitride is the "blue" in Blu-ray discs.

Anyone seen my spoon?

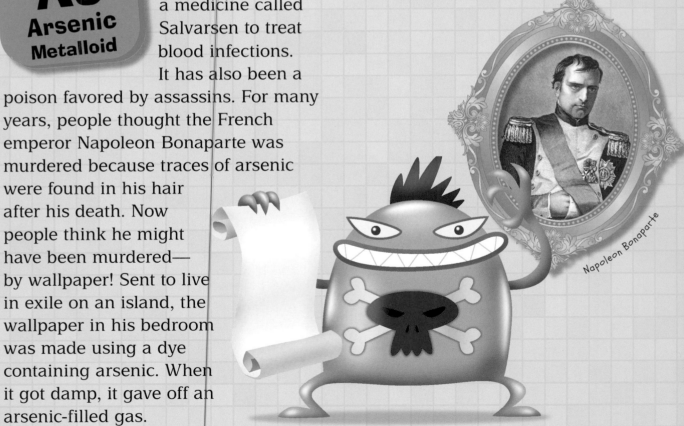

Atomic number 32

Ge
Germanium
Metalloid

The metalloid Germanium is named after Germany. This is another element that Mendeleev predicted would be found. It was first discovered in silver ore and can be extracted during the production of zinc. Germanium was used as one of the first **semiconductors**. In its inorganic form, it is sold in some countries as a nutritional supplement, even though it is actually harmful!

Atomic number 33

As
Arsenic
Metalloid

Although arsenic is highly toxic, it was once used in a medicine called Salvarsen to treat blood infections. It has also been a poison favored by assassins. For many years, people thought the French emperor Napoleon Bonaparte was murdered because traces of arsenic were found in his hair after his death. Now people think he might have been murdered— by wallpaper! Sent to live in exile on an island, the wallpaper in his bedroom was made using a dye containing arsenic. When it got damp, it gave off an arsenic-filled gas.

Atomic number 34

Se
Selenium
Non-Metal

Although it is silvery and shiny, like a lot of metals, selenium is a non-metal. Its name comes from the Greek word *selene*, meaning the moon. You are most likely to come across selenium in your bathroom, where it is used in anti-dandruff shampoos.

Napoleon Bonaparte

Atomic number 35

Br
Bromine
Non-Metal

The name bromine means "stench" in Greek. Pure bromine is a liquid at room temperature. It's usually found in the form of bromine salts in seawater and some mineral springs. If you were very rich in ancient times, you might have had your clothes dyed Tyrian purple, using a **pigment** with bromine, extracted from a type of sea snail. Yuck!

Atomic number 37

Rb
Rubidium
Metal

Rubidium is such a reactive metal that it will burst into flames in the air if you don't store it under oil. It is also mildly radioactive and can be used to give a purple color to fireworks.

Atomic number 38

Sr
Strontium
Metal

Strontium was named after the Scottish village of Strontian, where it was discovered. It has a very harmful radioactive **isotope**, called strontium-90. Huge areas in Chernobyl, Russia, were contaminated by strontium-90 in a nuclear disaster in 1986.

Atomic number 39

Y
Yttrium
Metal

Yttrium is used to make lasers and **superconductors**, as well as in cancer treatments. The isotope yttrium-90 can be used to make needles that are more precise than surgical scalpels. The needles are used for delicate spinal surgery.

Atomic number 40

Zr
Zirconium
Metal

If you can't afford to buy a diamond, zirconium is the next best thing. Zirconium itself is a soft gray metal, but when zirconium dioxide forms crystals, it looks just like diamonds.

Atomic number 41

Nb
Niobium
Metal

Niobium is a metal that reacts with oxygen, creating different colors. This makes it a great metal to use to make commemorative coins. For example, no two coins in the 2011 Full Moon coin sets produced in Canada are exactly alike, because each one was combined with oxygen differently.

Atomic number 42

Mo
Molybdenum
Metal

Due to a mixup, the name molybdenum comes from the Greek word for lead. This is because people used to confuse the ore containing molybdenum with the ore containing lead. Molybdenum was used in armor plating on tanks in World War I.

In the body, molybdenum is found in tooth enamel.

Atomic number 43

Tc
Technetium
Metal

Technetium is another one of Mendeleev's missing elements. After many false alarms, its existence was finally confirmed in 1936. It is a radioactive metal, mostly made inside nuclear reactors. It is used in medical equipment such as the SPECT scanner, which can show a 3-D image of your organs.

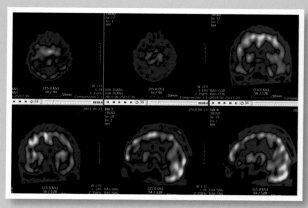

SPECT scan.

Atomic number 44

Ru
Ruthenium
Metal

One of the rarest metals on Earth, ruthenium is very resistant to corrosion. It is sometimes used as very thin plating on much cheaper metals, and may soon be used in solar cells and data storage systems.

Atomic number 46

Pd
Palladium
Metal

Like rhodium, the silvery-white metal called palladium is used in catalytic converters. It is also used to make an alloy of gold, called white gold, for use in jewelry.

Atomic number 48

Cd
Cadmium
Metal

You might still have rechargeable batteries in your house that contain nickel and cadmium. But beware—cadmium is hugely toxic to humans and to the environment. Those batteries are now being replaced by less toxic ones. Without this metal, however, French artist Claude Monet couldn't have created his famous pictures. One of his favorite colors was cadmium yellow.

Atomic number 45

Rh
Rhodium
Metal

Almost 80% of the rhodium that is produced worldwide is used in pollution-control devices, called catalytic converters, on cars. It is also a precious metal, and is sometimes used to symbolize great wealth or honor. To recognize his place in history as the bestselling recording artist and songwriter of all time, the Guinness Book of World Records gave Paul McCartney a rhodium plated disc in 1979.

Paul McCartney

Atomic number 47

Ag
Silver
Metal

Silver was first used in Egypt over 5,000 years ago. Since its discovery it has been used in a variety of ways, such as in mirrors and in jewelry. Before the invention of digital cameras, silver was used in photographic film. Silver salts are light-sensitive and will change to silver when exposed to light. This made a pattern of light and dark, which could be processed into a black-and-white photograph. Today, light-sensitive silver salts are used in the lenses of photo-reactive sunglasses. As it gets brighter outside, the silver salts react to the light, and the lenses become darker.

Mirrors

The first mirrors were sheets of polished metal, such as bronze or silver. These evolved into "looking glasses," which were first used in the Middle Ages. They were made from glass with silver foil behind it. Today, the silver is chemically bonded to the glass to make mirrors more durable.

Silver nitrate

Silver nitrate was once used as an antiseptic because silver is deadly to many bacteria and viruses. Today, it is put in some paints to make antibacterial surfaces.

Silver linings in clouds

The saying, "Every cloud has a silver lining" just might be true. Dropping silver iodide from aircraft or firing it from rockets into clouds is a method of trying to produce rain, called cloud seeding.

Indium is used in LCD screens

Atomic number 49

In
Indium
Metal

Indium is not named for India, but rather for the Latin word for the color indigo. It's used in LCD televisions, liquid crystals, and solar cells. Unfortunately, it's running out fast. We may only have 20 years supply left. Weirdly, if you bend a piece of indium, it screams! The sound comes from the crystals rearranging themselves.

Atomic number 50

Sn
Tin
Metal

Tin screams too, if you break a bar of it. Tin is used for coating steel to make tin cans because it doesn't get corroded by acidic food. In the 1800s, pewter, which is an alloy of lead and tin, was widely used for drinking cups and plates until lead was found to be toxic.

Atomic number 52

Te
Tellurium
Metalloid

Tellurium is very rare on Earth. It is used in the making of DVD and Blu-ray discs. It's toxic, and someone poisoned with tellurium smells like they have garlic breath. (Of course, so does someone eating garlic bread!)

Atomic number 51

Sb
Antimony
Metalloid

Antimony is toxic and was often used to get rid of "inconvenient" relatives in the 1800s. Some people think that it was used to poison the composer Mozart, who died in 1791. However, if you get the dose right, antimony can be used as a **laxative**. In the Middle Ages, antimony pills could be bought as re-useable laxatives— swallow one, then wait for it to "reappear." Yuck!

Mozart

Atomic number 53

I
Iodine
Non-Metal

Iodine compounds can be isolated easily from ocean water. It is vital to humans and many other animals. The body needs it to make chemicals that control how food is broken down in order to release energy. Iodine is used by the thyroid gland in your neck to make important chemical messengers. If you don't get enough, this gland grows extra big and leads to a condition called goiter. Nowadays iodine is added to table salt. Before that, the only way to get enough was by eating fish from the ocean. Before refrigerated trucks, you probably didn't get enough idodine if you lived a long way from the ocean.

Atomic number 55

Cs
Cesium
Metal

Cesium is a spectacularly reactive element that explodes in water! It has to be stored under oil and handled in a non-reactive atmosphere. Large quantities of its radioactive isotope, Cs-137, were released into the atmosphere by the explosion at the Chernobyl Nuclear Power Plant in 1986. Spread by the wind across huge areas of Europe, it contaminated soil and affected livestock. However, cesium does have its uses. If you want to know the time really accurately, consult an atomic clock. These clocks depend on atomic changes in cesium to work.

If you were a witch in the Middle Ages and wanted to impress other witches, what you really needed were some Bologna stones. These pebbles contain barite, a compound of barium. They would glow in the dark for days if you left them out in the sun for one day. Medical patients are often given barium to drink before x-rays. It helps outline the stomach and intestines in the scan.

Atomic number 56

Ba
Barium
Metal

The lanthanides

The lanthanides are a group of elements that live in a kind of "basement apartment" at the bottom of the periodic table. They share many properties and are found in the same areas. Many of them were discovered in samples of rock near the village of Ytterby in Sweden.

Atomic number 57
La
Lanthanum
Metal

Lanthanum metal is never found in its pure form. It took a hundred years for someone to even figure out how to purify it. Among its many uses are making nickel-hydride batteries for **hybrid** cars and clearing algae from ponds.

Atomic number 58
Ce
Cerium
Metal

Cerium looks a little like iron, but it is much softer. Shavings of cerium will burst into flames on contact with air. It is used in catalytic converters.

SLOW

Atomic number 59
Pr
Praseodymium
Metal

Praseodymium can be used to color glass and enamel yellow. It also makes up part of a special glass that can slow the speed of light to a few hundred meters per second instead of 299,792,458 meters per second.

Atomic number 60
Nd
Neodymium
Metal

Neodymium is used to make some of the strongest magnets you can find. A neodymium magnet can lift 1,000 times its weight.

Atomic number 61
Pm
Promethium
Metal

Highly radioactive, promethium hardly ever occurs naturally. It can be made in a lab and is used to make luminous paint.

Atomic number 62
Sm
Samarium
Metal

Samarium was discovered by French chemist Paul-Émile Lecoq de Boisbaudran in 1879. Its radioactive isotope, samarium-153, is used in the treatment of cancer.

Atomic number 63
Eu
Europium
Metal

Named after the continent, Europium doesn't have many uses now. It was mainly used for making early color televisions in the 1960s.

Atomic number 64

Gd
Gadolinium
Metal

Gadolinium is very good at absorbing neutrons, so it is used as shielding in nuclear reactors. It is also magnetic, but only up to 66° F (19° C).

Atomic number 65

Tb
Terbium
Metal

Pure terbium is soft, silvery-white, and very expensive—four times as costly as platinum. Its most interesting use is in a device that can transform an entire flat surface of metal or wood into a speaker when it is attached to it.

Atomic number 66

Dy
Dysprosium
Metal

The name dysprosium means "hard to get"— and it is. Although it's a metal, it's so soft that you can cut it with an ordinary knife. It's needed to make motors for electric cars and is an important ingredient in clean energy technologies.

Atomic number 67

Ho
Holmium
Metal

Holmium gets its name from the city of Stockholm in Sweden. It has the highest magnetic strength of any element and is used in nuclear control rods, which control the power of a nuclear reactor.

Atomic number 68

Er
Erbium
Metal

Erbium reacts so easily with water or oxygen that it's never found as a pure metal. Your dentist might be using it if you have laser dentistry.

Atomic number 69

Tm
Thulium
Metal

Although it is a metal, thulium will catch fire at a lower temperature than paper! It is used in portable x-ray machines.

Atomic number 70

Yb
Ytterbium
Metal

Even though most ytterbium is extracted from clay in areas of China, it is named after the village of Ytterby in Sweden where it was first found. It is used in pressure gauges that measure explosions and earthquakes.

Atomic number 71

Lu
Lutetium
Metal

Lutetium is a very hard, dense metal. For a long time, it was the most costly element to isolate. It is still too rare and expensive to have many uses.

The rocket nozzle of the Apollo Lunar Module contains hafnium.

Atomic number 74

W
Tungsten
Metal

Tungsten is also known as wolfram, which means wolf's froth! This is because the people who processed the element's ore said that tungsten could devour tin the way that wolves devour sheep! Used by some bacteria, it is the heaviest element with a biological function. Until recently it was used for making the wire **filament** in light bulbs.

Atomic number 72

Hf
Hafnium
Metal

Hafnium was one of the last stable elements to be identified. This is because its chemical properties are so similar to zirconium that scientists found it very difficult to tell them apart. Hafnium is used in control rods in the pressurized water reactors of nuclear power plants.

Atomic number 73

Ta
Tantalum
Metal

Because it is resistant to rust, tantalum is sometimes used to make parts for very expensive watches. It is named after Tantalus, a figure in Greek mythology who was punished in the afterlife by having food and drink nearby, but always just out of reach.

Atomic number 75

Re
Rhenium
Metal

Found in 1925, rhenium was the last stable element to be discovered. Scientists had to process 1,455 pounds (660 kilograms) of molybdenite ore to get just 0.035 of an ounce (one gram) of rhenium. It is used in superalloys to make jet engine parts.

Atomic number 76

Os
Osmium
Metal

Osmium is the densest element and hardest metal. It gets its name from the Greek word *osme*, which means smell. So, it really should be called smellium! Osmium is the least abundant stable element in Earth's crust. It is used as a preservative for specimens being viewed through an electron microscope.

Atomic number 77

Ir
Iridium
Metal

Although iridium is rare on Earth, it is common in meteorites—including the one scientists think may have led to the extinction of the dinosaurs. Sixty-six million years ago, a meteorite over six miles (ten km) wide crashed to Earth in the Gulf of Mexico near the Yucatan peninsula. It left a crater about 186-miles (300 km) wide, as well as a layer of clay rich in iridium. When the meteorite struck, it sent up a huge dust cloud that blocked so much sunlight most plants could no longer carry out photosynthesis. The animals—including dinosaurs—who depended on these plants for food, died out.

Atomic number 78

Pt
Platinum
Metal

For at least 2,000 years, humans have used platinum to make jewelry. Today, platinum is used in catalytic converters and in cancer treatments, and is more valuable than gold. We describe a music record that sells more than one million copies as having "gone platinum." Interestingly, even though you can find platinum in some river sands, there was never a platinum rush to equal the silver and gold rushes of history. The International Prototype Kilogram (which describes the exact measure of a kilogram) is represented by a cylinder of platinum-iridium alloy made in 1879.

Atomic number 79

Au
Gold
Metal

The Latin word for gold is *aurum*, which is where the symbol Au comes from. Gold is a different color than most metals, which are usually gray or silvery-white. Gold gets its color from fast-moving electrons.

Gold is one of the rarest elements on Earth. Most of it exists in seawater, but it is too spread out to be collected there. It is popular for jewelry because it stays bright and untarnished indefinitely. The biggest nugget of gold ever found was one called Welcome Stranger. Mined in Victoria, Australia, in 1858, it weighed an impressive 158 pounds (72 kg)!

The California Gold Rush
Between 1848 and 1855, a gold rush brought 300,000 people to California. San Francisco was a village of 200 people when the rush started and quickly grew to 36,000 by 1852. Gold rushes also took place in Alaska, the Yukon in Canada, Australia, and South Africa.

Preparing the fields for the gold extraction

Here are some more nuggets of information about gold.

Panning for gold

Panning is an ancient way of extracting gold from river gravel. Water is swirled over the gravel in a special shallow pan. Since gold is heavy, it sinks to the bottom of the pan while the lighter materials are washed out of it.

The legend of the Golden Fleece

A Greek myth tells the story of the hero Jason, who stole the Golden Fleece. The gold-colored wool was the symbol of the king. Some people think the story might have been based on a method of finding gold in rivers. By suspending a sheep's fleece in the water, gold caught in the wool might make it look golden.

What is a karat?

The purity of gold is measured in karats. Something that is made of pure gold has a measure of 24 karats. Eighteen-karat gold means that, out of the full 24 parts, 18 parts are gold and the remaining 6 parts are other metals.

Not the vegetable!

Hg
Mercury
Metal

The old name for mercury was quicksilver. Its symbol comes from the Latin word *hydragyrum*, which means liquid silver. It is the only metal that is a liquid at room temperature. In fact, the only other element that is liquid at room temperature is bromine. Mercury is so dense that lead will float on it.

Thermometers used to contain mercury. Now, many contain alcohol instead because mercury is quite toxic. It's used in many types of mascara, and in the material used to fill cavities in teeth—but, don't worry, it isn't a toxic amount. It also used to be in a lot of medicines before people realized how harmful it was. Hundreds of years ago, the Moors in what is now Spain built palace gardens with mercury reflecting-pools in them. Visitors could dip their fingers in, which is not such a great idea, upon reflection!

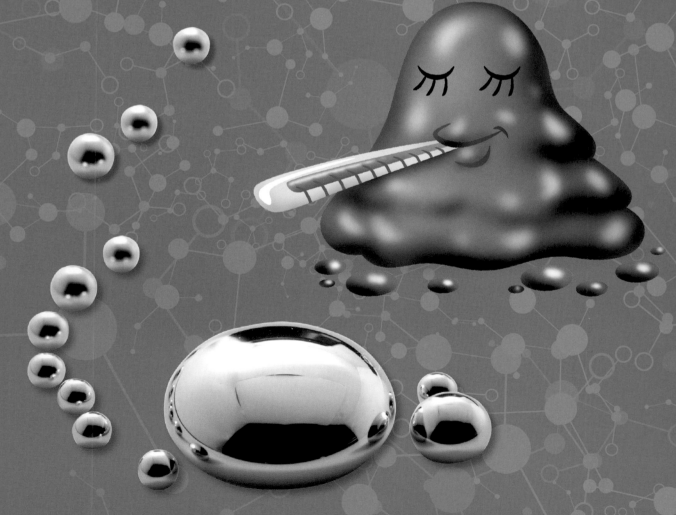

Minamata disease

Between 1932 and 1968, methylmercury was released into the sea through industrial wastewater near the city of Minamata in Japan. It contaminated the fish and shellfish eaten by the local people. The result was mercury poisoning. In humans, it caused numbness and damage to hearing and speech. In some cases, it even caused paralysis, insanity, coma, and death. Over 2,200 victims suffered from Minamata disease. Animals were also affected. In cats, it was known as "dancing cat fever" because of the way in which their movement was affected.

Mad as a hatter

If you have read *Alice in Wonderland*, you will have come across the Mad Hatter. Author Lewis Carroll didn't just dream this character up at random. In Victorian times, Mad Hatter Disease was well known. It was caused by the use of mercury compounds in the production of felt for fur hats.

Atomic number 81

Tl
Thallium
Metal

Thallium is known as "the poisoner's poison" because it was often used for murder. Thallium sulphate dissolves in water, has no taste or odor, and is hard to detect in the body. It was easy to buy because it used to be sold as rat poison.

Arrghh!

"Aunt Thally" Grills

One of Australia's most famous murder cases featured thallium poisoning. In 1953, 63-year-old Caroline Grills was convicted of killing four members of her family, and trying to kill another two, by putting thallium sulphate in their tea. In prison, she was nicknamed "Aunt Thally." This was just one of a series of thallium murders in Australia at that time.

Spoiler alert!

Author Agatha Christie used thallium as the murder weapon in her book *The Pale Horse*. In doing so, she also saved some real lives. At least two readers recognized the symptoms of thallium poisoning in other people after reading the book!

Agatha Christie

Atomic number 83

Bi
Bismuth
Metal

Bismuth is a silvery-pink metal, obtained mostly as a by-product in the production of copper and tin. It is probably best known as an ingredient in some treatments for stomach problems.

Bismuth is also used as a pigment in nail polish and eye shadow.

Atomic number 85

At
Astatine
Metal

One of the rarest elements on Earth, astatine has never actually been seen! This is because a piece big enough to be seen would instantly vaporize in the heat generated by its own radioactivity. Probably less than 0.035 of an ounce (1 g) exists on Earth at any time.

Atomic number 87

Fr
Francium
Metal

The most unstable of the natural elements, francium is almost impossible to investigate. As a result, not a lot is known about it, and it doesn't have any **commercial uses**.

Atomic number 82

Pb
Lead
Metal

Lead is the heaviest metal and gets its symbol from the Latin word *plumbum*. Put that together with the fact that most water pipes used to be made of lead, and you'll see why we call it plumbing.

Lead pipes seemed like a good idea at the time. Lead is easy to mold and bend, so you could make pipes that go around corners. However, it turned out that lead is toxic, and lead pipes made people sick. Copper, steel, and plastic are used now to make pipes. Lead has had various uses for thousands of years because it is easy to obtain and to work.

Let me lead you through some facts about lead…

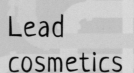

Queen Elizabeth I

Lead cosmetics

It's amazing what people will put on their faces. In the past, people used white lead in powders and pastes to give them a fashionably pale complexion, even though they knew it could lead to bad skin, baldness, and even death!

Lead pigments

Lead pigments used to be used in paint, but not anymore, for obvious reasons. It was a particularly bad idea to paint a baby's crib with lead paint because babies sometimes chew on the bars when they are teething.

Thomas Midgley

In 1921, American engineer Thomas Midgley discovered that adding a little tetraethyl lead to gasoline made car engines work much better. Gasoline manufacturers began adding it to their product. It took a long time for manufacturers to realize that the signs of poisoning many of their workers were showing were connected to the added lead. By the 1970s, lead was phased out after scientists identified it as a major pollutant, affecting humans and the environment. Now, most gasoline is lead-free.

Unfortunately for Thomas Midgley, he may hold the record for doing more harm to the environment than any other human being. He is also responsible for developing chemicals known as chlorofluorocarbons, or CFCs for short, which were widely used in refrigeration, aerosol spray cans, and Styrofoam packaging. When released into the atmosphere, these chemicals head straight for the ozone layer and hang around for thousands of years, constantly damaging it.

The Franklin Expedition

In 1845, British Captain Sir John Franklin led a voyage of exploration to the Arctic. They set out from England but were never seen again. Searchers eventually found several graves of crew members. Studies of the bodies showed high levels of lead. At first, it was assumed they had been poisoned by the lead which was used to seal up cans of food. However, since lead was a commonly used metal back then, it is now thought that most people bodies' contained high levels of lead.

Pierre Curie

Marie Curie

Atomic number 84

Po
Polonium
Metalloid

Deadly, poisonous polonium was discovered by Marie and Pierre Curie in 1898. The couple named it after their native country of Poland in order to bring attention to Poland's lack of independence at the time. The first death from polonium poisoning may have been the Curies' daughter Irene Joliot-Curie. She died from leukemia some years after a capsule of polonium exploded on the bench where she was working.

Marie and Pierre Curie

Marie and Pierre Curie spent years studying uranium ore. They found that it contained other elements, too—radium and polonium. In 1903, they were awarded the Nobel Prize for Physics, along with Henri Becquerel, for their discoveries. Marie was the first woman ever to win a Nobel Prize. Pierre died in 1906.

In 1911, Marie was awarded another Nobel Prize. This prize was in chemistry for her work on radium. She developed x-ray machines that could be carried by ambulance to wounded soldiers on the battlefields during World War I. She died in 1934 of aplastic anemia, an illness she likely developed from her exposure to radiation during her work. Even now, Marie Curie's notebooks are so radioactive they have to be kept in lead-lined boxes and only be handled by people in protective clothing.

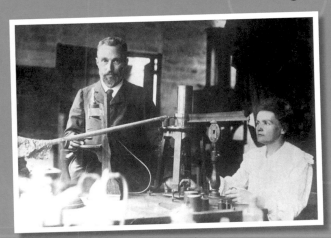

Marie and Pierre Curie working in a laboratory

Assassinations

Polonium has been suspected in assassinations, including the death of Russian secret service officer Alexander Litvinenko in 2006. Litvinenko accused the Russian government of murder, and then fled to England. In London, he became ill and died a slow, painful death. Investigators found polonium in his body and in places he had been before falling ill.

Atomic number 88

Ra
Radium
Metal

The Curies discovered radium in 1898. It is radioactive and glows in the dark. The use of radium became very popular in the early 1900s, before people realized the dangers. It was used to make glowing paint and to make watch dials glow. It was painted on watches by workers, called "Radium Girls," who often licked their brushes to give them a nice, fine point.

Not surprisingly, the girls often became ill. More bizarrely, it was added to toothpaste, hair creams, and health drinks. Radium was also used as an important treatment for cancers.

Atomic number 89

Ac
Actinium
Metal

Actinium is extracted from uranium ore. This is quite a difficult job, since there is only about 0.2 milligrams of actinium in one ton of ore! Because it is so scarce and highly radioactive, it has no commercial uses.

Atomic number 91

Pa
Protactinium
Metal

Very rare, very toxic, and almost entirely useless, protactinium can be extracted—with great difficulty—from uranium ore. However, 60 tons (54 metric tons) of uranium would only give you about 4.4 ounces (125 g) of protactinium!

Atomic number 90

Th
Thorium
Metal

Thorium is named after Thor, the Norse god of thunder. Some countries are researching whether this radioactive element could be used in nuclear reactors instead of uranium.

The Manhattan Project

The research project that developed the first atomic bombs during World War II was codenamed the Manhattan Project. It involved the United States, the United Kingdom, and Canada. Work was carried out at more than 30 sites in those three countries. Beginning in 1939, it led to the production of two types of atomic bombs: one containing uranium and the other plutonium. The project also had secret agents who monitored the enemy's research into nuclear weapons in Germany. The first ever nuclear explosion was the Trinity Test, carried out in New Mexico. After the test, the scientific director of the project, J. Robert Oppenheimer, famously quoted Hindu scripture, saying, "Now I am become death, the destroyer of worlds." Near the end of the war, two nuclear bombs were dropped on Japan, the only nuclear weapons ever to have been used. Research continued until 1947.

Atomic bomb explosion

Atomic number 92

U

Uranium
Metal

The best known of the radioactive elements, uranium is used in nuclear reactors to supply electricity in many countries. Amazingly, it has been discovered that uranium deposits in Gabon, West Africa, had acted as natural nuclear reactors. Known as the Oklo Fossil Reactors, they were active 1.7 billion years ago!

Before people realized uranium was radioactive, it was used in coatings on tile and pottery. Its radioactivity was discovered when French physicist Henri Becquerel put a sample of uranium salts into a drawer on top of a photographic plate. When he looked at it later, he found that the plate had been fogged by the uranium's radioactivity.

Nuclear power plant

Atomic bombs

The destructive use of uranium in atomic bombs is well known. Powered by uranium, the first atomic bomb, called "Little Boy," was dropped in World War II on the city of Hiroshima, Japan, on August 6, 1945. Many people died in the first few days after the bombing but, over the next few months, many more died of radiation sickness. The plutonium-powered "Fat Man" was dropped next on the city of Nagasaki. Experts believe about 275,000 people were killed in the bombings.

Fictional elements

Science fiction often makes up new elements. You've already met Kryptonite. Here are some more fictional elements.

Dilithium

The crystals that regulate the Star Ship Enterprise's warp engines in *Star Trek*

Octiron

A dense, black metal found in the crust of Terry Pratchett's book *Discworld*

Unobtainium

The fantastically rare metal being mined on the planet Pandora in the film *Avatar*

Mithril

A light, strong, silvery metal used by elves to make the mail shirts worn by Bilbo and Frodo Baggins in books *The Hobbit* and *The Lord of the Rings*

Carbonite

Han Solo is frozen into a block of carbonite at the end of the *Star Wars* film, *The Empire Strikes Back*.

And finally, elements that don't exist but really should

Yummium
Chemical symbol: Mmm
The tastiest element of them all

Amazonium
An element only available online

Gymnasium
Often added to muscle-building supplements

A quick guide to particles

Subatomic particles are protons, neutrons, and electrons. Together these make up an...

Atom—the basic unit of an element. It can't be broken down any further by a chemical reaction. Atoms join together to make a...

Molecule—two or more atoms joined by chemical bonds. For example, an oxygen molecule is O_2—two atoms of oxygen stuck together. Water is H_2O—two atoms of hydrogen combined with one atom of oxygen.
This is called a...

Compound—a substance made of molecules of two or more elements

I'm very particular about paricles.

The Complete Periodic Table

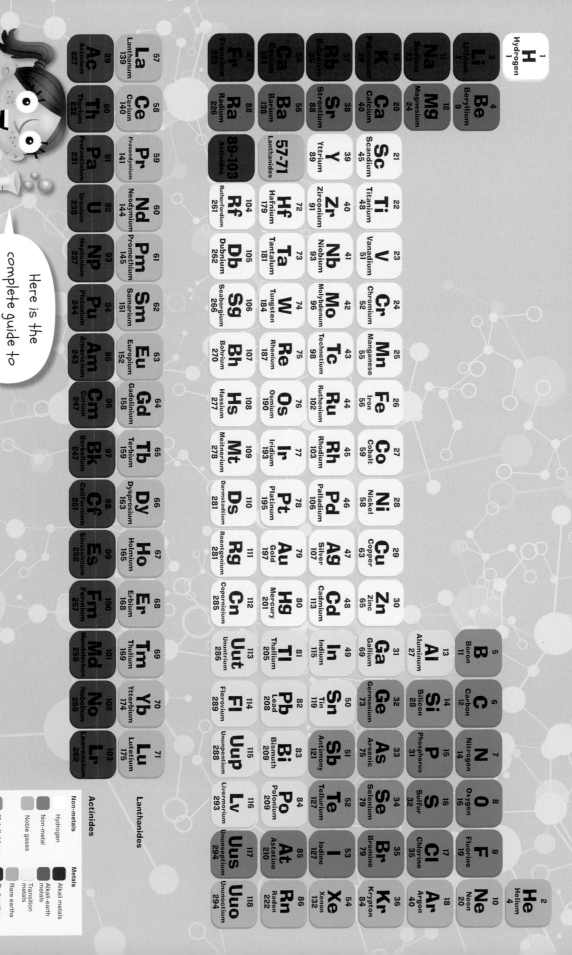

Here is the complete guide to the periodic table

Find Out More

Read

"Why Chemistry Matters" series (Crabtree Publishing, 2009)

Mendeleev on the Periodic Law: Selected Writings, 1869-1905 (Dover Publications, 2012)

What Makes You YOU? by Gill Arbuthnott (Crabtree Publishing, 2016)

Watch

With the help of a fun song, this video teaches viewers about the different elements of the periodic table.
www.sciencekids.co.nz/videos/chemistry/elementsong.html

Visit this website for videos and fun games about the periodic table.
www.neok12.com/Periodic-Table.htm

Visit

The Sterling Hills Mining Museum in New Jersey has opened a new exhibit that studies the periodic table of elements.
http://sterlinghillminingmuseum.org/periodictable/index.php

The University of Waterloo Earth Sciences Museum in Ontario offers a close look at rocks, minerals, and precious stones.
https://uwaterloo.ca/earth-sciences-museum/

Log on to

Find out more about the elements of the periodic table at:
www.chem4kids.com/files/elem_intro.html

Test your knowledge of the elements with this great interactive quiz at
www.chem4kids.com/extras/quiz_elemintro/index.html

Get detailed information on the periodic table of elements, and then test out your knowledge with a quiz or activity at:
www.bbc.co.uk/education/guides/z84wjxs/revision

Glossary

Note: Some boldfaced words are defined where they appear in the text.

Abundant Exists in a very large quantity

Alchemist Someone who studied alchemy, which was what existed before proper, scientific chemistry. Alchemy was a combination of chemistry and magic.

Alloy A metal melted together with another element, which often makes it stronger. Bronze is an alloy of copper and tin.

Climate change The warming of Earth's temperature due to human-made pollution

Commercial use Use of something in order to make money. For instance, one commercial use of aluminum is to make soft drink cans.

Conductor A material that carries (conducts) electricity

Cosmic rays Particles from space that are very highly charged with energy. They strike and sometimes penetrate Earth's atmosphere, interacting with its elements.

Filament A very thin, threadlike structure, in this case made of wire that conducts electric energy in light bulbs

Fossil fuel Any fuel that is formed by natural processes (from plant or animal remains), such as coal, gas, and oil

Galvanize Coating a metal with zinc in order to protect it from corrosion

Hybrid Something that has two different parts that can perform the same function

Incubator A machine that has controlled conditions, such as temperature, oxygen levels, and humidity. Used to help living things, in this case sick or premature babies, grow.

Isolated Separated from another substance

Isotopes Forms of the same element with different numbers of neutrons in the nucleus. For example, strontium has 50 neutrons, but radioactive strontium-90 has 52.

Large Hadron Collider A huge particle accelerator in Switzerland. It is used to smash particles—beams of protons, for instance—into each other at great speed to test theories about physics and try to find evidence for the existence of fundamental particles.

Laxative A medicine used to make it easier to empty your bowels (in other words, something that makes you poo)

Metalloid An element with properties of both a metal and a non-metal

Ore Mineral from which metal is extracted

Photosynthesis The process by which plants use energy from sunlight to convert water and carbon dioxide into sugars

Pigment A substance used to give something color

Reactive Describing something that quickly responds or changes when exposed to something else; a stimulus

Salary A wage that is paid monthly. From the Latin word for salt—*sal*—as Roman soldiers got part of their pay to buy salt

Semiconductors A substance or element that is both a conductor and an insulator, or both holds and carries energy

Smelt Melt ore in order to produce metal

Subatomic Part of an atom

Superconductors A substance that is able to conduct energy perfectly, without any resistance, at temperatures close to absolute zero

Three-dimensional (3-D) Having or seeming to have width, height, and depth

Toxic Poisonous

Ultraviolet (UV) radiation Invisible rays that are part of the energy that comes from the Sun. They are part of the electromagnetic spectrum, which also includes x-rays and radio waves.

Unreactive Describing something that does not respond or change when exposed to a stimuli

Index